Contents

Introduction

This book is intended to have a wide appeal - to help new residents and visitors to familiarise themselves with this lovely region, to encourage existing local residents to explore their area further, or just for enjoyment and as a way to keep fit and healthy. Each walk has a shorter option for those with less time or energy but also intended to entice non walkers into the countryside and, perhaps, inspire them to take up more regular walking.

Some of the walks are in the unique and spectacular landscape of the North Wessex Downs 'Area of Outstanding Natural Beauty' (AONB) which includes tranquil open downland, ancient woodlands and chalk streams. There are many nature reserves to be found in this area and the attractive river valleys of the Kennet, the Dun, the Lambourn and the Enborne are central to the walks of this book. The Kennet & Avon Canal, which twines its way along and beside the rivers, is an extra feature of interest and a convenient and attractive way of moving through the countryside and the urban areas. Where there is space on the maps points of interest are indicated but there are many more to discover in the rich heritage of our landscape. Although the walks start mainly in urban areas it is remarkable how quickly the attractive countryside in this area can be reached, even on foot.

Car parks have been included but all the walks can be reached by bus and the majority of them are served by the railway. Railway stations and relevant bus routes are shown on each walk with further details of public transport given on page 3.

The terrain in this area is not particularly demanding but walking shoes or boots are advisable especially after a spell of wet weather.

It is important to use the text in conjunction with the maps when following the walks. The maps are simplified but accurate copies of the Ordnance Survey Explorer series, mainly sheets 158 and 159 but with two walks on sheet 157.
To assist in following the routes, on the maps *and alongside the written directions* -
short walk routes are shown with short lines, long routes with long lines and combined routes with alternate long and short lines.

The preparation of this book has given much enjoyment to many members of the West Berkshire Ramblers and we trust that when you are using it you will gain as much pleasure as we did.

Public Transport

Public Transport can be used to reach the start of most of the walks and, in the case of bus services, other points on many of the walks enabling them to be shortened if desired.
It is advisable to verify times before traveling as timetables are liable to change at short notice or may be affected by engineering works, especially at weekends.

Trains

A local service operates from Reading to Bedwyn (Great Bedwyn) serving Theale, Aldermaston, Midgham (Woolhampton), Thatcham, Newbury Racecourse, Newbury, Kintbury and Hungerford. These services may originate from either London Paddington or Reading. Some services terminate at Newbury and it is mainly these that call at Aldermaston, Midgham and Newbury Racecourse. Numerous other railway services operate to or via Reading enabling connections to be made onto Bedwyn line trains. Timetable leaflets are available from staffed stations, also times are posted at all stations. Alternatively telephone 08457 484950 or visit www.nationalrail.co.uk.

Buses

A complex network of bus services operates throughout the area covered by the walks. In rural areas most buses will stop anywhere where it is safe to do so; just tell the driver when you want to get off or hail a bus if you wish to board. In towns and most villages there are bus stops. The maps show the bus services that operate in the vicinity of each walk. Timetables may be obtained from West Berkshire Council offices in Market Street and Faraday Road, Newbury, also the Tourist Information office in Wharf Street. Many libraries also keep stocks. Times of services that operate in Berkshire may also be obtained from the Transport Services Team at West Berkshire Council on 01635 503248 who can also post timetables to you. For services in Wiltshire contact Wiltshire Council on 01225 713004. There is also a national organization known as "Traveline" which provides public transport and timetable information, including a journey planner, on its website, www.traveline.co.uk, or can be contacted on 0871 200 2233 (extended hours).

Bus Operators:

Service	Operator	Telephone No.
1, 4, 6, 6A, 7, 8, 11, 12, 13, 15	Newbury Buses	01635 567500
2, 3A, 3B, 3C, 101, 104, 105, 107	Newbury & District (Weavaway)	01635 33855
H1, 95	Jacs Minicoach Travel	01635 582929
X2, 20(Wilts) 20A, 22, 22A	Wilts & Dorset	01722 336855
20(Berks) X20, The Link	Stagecoach in Hampshire	0845 1210190
C21, C22, C23, C24	Cango	0845 6024135
46	Thamesdown Transport	01793 428428
75	D.J. Travel	0118 9333725
222	Tourist Coaches	01722 338359

Follow the Countryside Code

By following The Countryside Code you will get the best enjoyment possible from your walk and you will help to protect the countryside now and for future generations.

Be Safe - Plan ahead and follow any signs -
Even when going out locally, it's best to get the latest information about where and when you can go; for example, your rights to go to some areas of open land may be restricted while work is carried out, for safety reasons or during the breeding season. Follow advice and local signs and be prepared for the unexpected.

Leave gates and property as you find them -
Please respect the working life of the countryside as our actions can affect people's livelihoods, our heritage and the safety and welfare of animals and ourselves.

Protect plants and animals and take your litter home -
We have a responsibility to protect our countryside now and for future generations, so make sure you don't harm animals, birds, plants or trees.

Keep dogs under close control -
The countryside is a great place to exercise dogs but it's every owner's duty to make sure their dog is not a danger or a nuisance to farm animals, wildlife or other people.

Consider other people -
Showing consideration and respect for other people makes the countryside a pleasant environment for everyone - at home, at work and at leisure.

Acknowledgements

Project Co-ordinator: Fiona Walker.
Routes devised by: Fred Carter, Ray Clayton, Colin Honeybone, Geoff Vince and
                         Fiona Walker.
Maps and Graphics: Geoff Vince.
Public Transport: Paul Frances.
Published by: West Berks Ramblers.

Thanks also to all members who checked the routes, maps and directions.

Rights of Way

The majority of paths used in these walks are Public Rights of Way. These are indicated with fingerposts and waymarks as shown. The arrow shows the direction of the path whilst its colour shows who may use the path, as below.

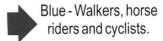 Yellow - Walkers only.

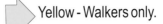 Blue - Walkers, horse riders and cyclists.

Red - all the above and vehicles.

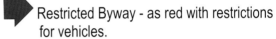 Restricted Byway - as red with restrictions for vehicles.

A Waymark

Finger post

On the walk directions 'path' and 'footpath' have been used as generic descriptions and may include any of the above whether specified or not.

Some paths are 'Permitted Paths'. These may or may not be signed or may have 'Walkers Welcome' waymarks as shown. Permitted paths may be closed by the landowner with little notice.

Under the Countryside and Rights of Way Act a measure called 'The Right to Roam' was introduced. This right applies only to walkers and only to specified areas. It does not apply generally to private land, agricultural land or farm tracks.

Key to symbols used on the walk maps.

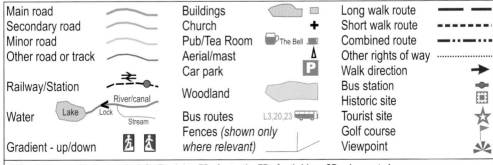

Main road		Buildings		Long walk route	
Secondary road		Church	+	Short walk route	
Minor road		Pub/Tea Room	The Bell	Combined route	
Other road or track		Aerial/mast		Other rights of way	
		Car park	P	Walk direction	
Railway/Station		Woodland		Bus station	
	River/canal			Historic site	
Water	Lake Lock	Bus routes	L3,20,23	Tourist site	
	Stream	Fences (shown only		Golf course	
Gradient - up/down		where relevant)		Viewpoint	

Abbreviations used in the text: **L - left,** **R - right,** **FP - footpath,** **FB - footbridge,** **SP - signposted,** *Incidental information is shown in italics*

NB - the symbols identifying the three route styles are repeated to the left of the directions paragraphs to assist walkers to follow the correct instructions.

Walk 1

Crofton Beam Engines

Start - Great Bedwyn Station
(Parking places shown
on the map.)

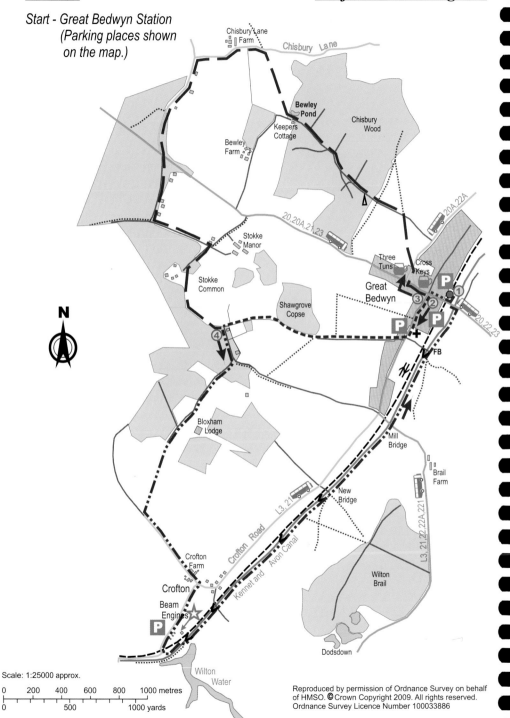

Chisbury Lane Farm

Chisbury Lane

Bewley Pond

Chisbury Wood

Keepers Cottage

Bewley Farm

20.20A.21.23

Stokke Manor

Three Tuns

Cross Keys

20A.22A

Stokke Common

Great Bedwyn

Shawgrove Copse

20.22.23

FB

Bloxham Lodge

Mill Bridge

Brail Farm

New Bridge

Crofton Road

L3.21

L3. 21.22.22A.221

Crofton Farm

Wilton Brail

Crofton
Beam Engines

Kennet and Avon Canal

Dodsdown

Wilton Water

N

Scale: 1:25000 approx.

0   200   400   600   800   1000 metres

0   500   1000 yards

① From the station walk up to the road, turn R towards the village.

Short walk para - 2   Long walk para - 3

② Turn L into Church Street. At St. Mary's church turn R into Shawgrove. On the bend turn R at FP sign and enter field. Follow FP past Shawgrove Copse on R, over the stile and continue to follow fence on L. Go over stile and exit field through gate on L just past cottage on L. Follow path to track immediately in front and turn L.

Go to paragraph 4

③ Turn R in front of The Three Tuns into Brown's Lane. After 100m turn L at FP sign into a field. Head diagonally R towards the telegraph pole on FP leading to the mast. Follow FP signs straight through Chisbury Wood passing between Keepers Cottage

The Kennet and Avon Canal at Crofton

on L and Bewley Pond on R as you emerge into a field and head diagonally R heading well to the R of Chisbury Lane Farm. Cross a stile onto road and turn L. At junction turn L and then at cross roads continue ahead passing cottages on L. At path T junction turn L. At Stokke Common, by large birch tree on R, take R fork. At a 'Children's Play' sign fork L then bear R in front of a cottage with high fences.

Go to paragraph 4

Crofton Pumping Station

④ Continue ahead to pass a red letterbox by a cottage on L then down at junction turn R at waymark. Follow fence on L keeping L onto bridleway with stock fence on L until end of wood where you pass through a pedestrian steel gate. Follow FP keeping hedge on R to see the chimney of Crofton Beam Engine ahead on L. At the lane turn L to go through Crofton Farm and turn R at the T junction by Crofton Farmhouse. Continue along the road to turn into Crofton Pumping Station entrance on the L. (*Visit the beam engine at your leisure*). Pass through and cross the canal at the lock. Turn L and follow the towpath back to Great Bedwyn.

(*Should the beam engine be closed carry on over the railway bridge and turn L through a field gate onto a path following the canal*).

Walk 2   *Wilton Windmill*

Start - Great Bedwyn Station
     (Parking places shown on the map.)

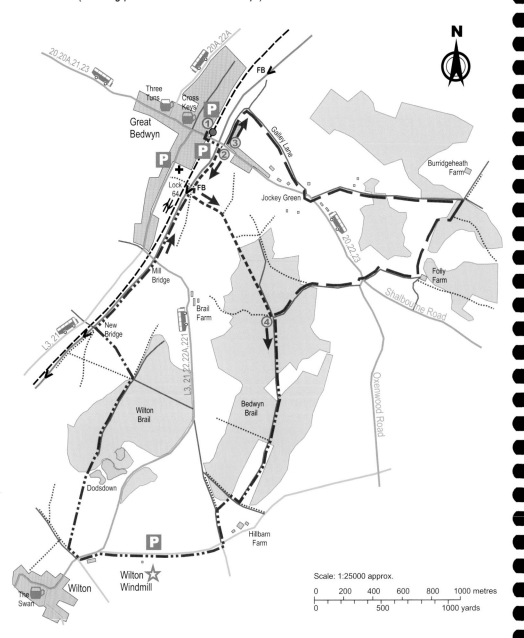

Scale: 1:25000 approx.

| 0 | 200 | 400 | 600 | 800 | 1000 metres |
| 0 | | 500 | | 1000 yards | |

① From the station walk up to the road, turn L away from the village and cross the canal.

Short walk para - 2   Long walk para - 3

② Turn into Bedwyn Wharf on the R. With the canal on your R follow the towpath for 400m to the bridge by lock 64. Turn L through gate by the bridge, follow path for 50m then cross stile on L. Follow the hedge uphill to enter the copse in corner of field. Follow path through copse and across clearing to merge with forestry track and come to a junction of paths. Go ahead.

Go to paragraph 4

③ Turn L into Frog Lane. After 300m turn R to Jockey Green. Pass houses on L and take L FP, signed Burridge Heath for 1km. Turn R in front of wood, pass byway on L and turn R in wood to clearing under telegraph wires. Go straight down field with fir trees on L straight up to waymark post. Turn R on a tarmac lane and come to Shalbourne Road. Cross this road and follow the Oxenwood Road L for 50m to turn R on FP to Bedwyn Brail. Keep L of pollarded oak and follow wood edge, bearing L on a wide, grassy path to a junction of paths. Turn L.

Go to paragraph 4

④ Take the path SP 'Windmill' for about half a mile passing a barn on the L and at a junction a sign to Wilton Brail on the R. At next crossing path take R track, SP 'Windmill' and after 40m bear L at second Windmill sign by a seat carved from a fallen tree. After 200m, at a T junction turn L to the road then turn R. Pass Wilton Windmill on

Wilton Windmill

your L. Continue 400m past cottage on L then take track on R SP 'Crofton Beam Engine'. After 100m turn R on narrow FP to a stile at field edge. Go across field heading for the tallest tree on L of tree line to a small clearing of the hedge. Follow FP into Dodsdown and Wilton Brail following waymark signs to a clearing and junction of paths. Turn L through a stile and take the middle path following fence line down the field to the canal. Turn R and follow the towpath* back to Great Bedwyn.

*(An alternative option is to turn L at lock 64, cross bridge towards St Mary's church and pass through churchyard into Church Street. Turn R through the village centre passing the Post Office and Lloyds Stonemasons museum then R to station).

Walk 3   *Standen Manor*

Start - Hungerford Station.
Parking - Station Road car park (pay & display) or Hungerford Common.

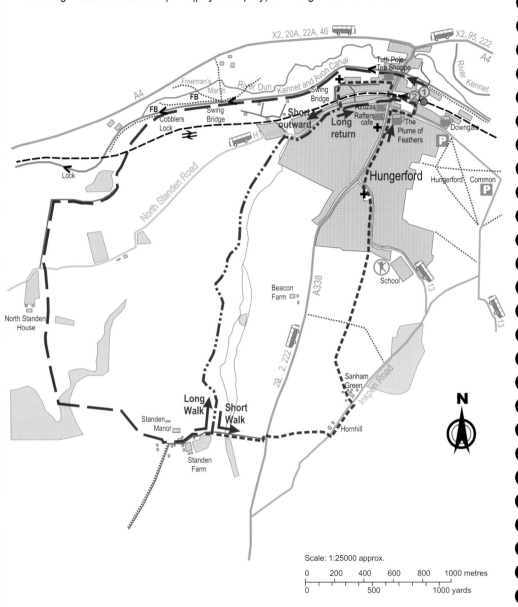

Scale: 1:25000 approx.

① **Long walk -** Leave the station by the vehicular exit. Cross the level crossing to join the canal towpath and turn L. Follow towpath to Cobblers Lock. Cross stile on L of towpath then turn R to follow FP to far R corner of field and cross the railway by the

The Canal at Hungerford Lock

steps. Cross stile and follow FP to the R. At T junction turn L onto a track. Just before reaching road take small FP to L, cross road and take FP opposite which turns sharp L through woodland then crosses a field to reach Standen Farm and Manor. Keep the Manor on L and just past the house, by a very ornate gate is a path on your L. Turn L across a stile, cross a field to another stile and continue on field edge keeping trees to your R. Where path turns sharp L take path on R through the hedge to cross a stile and bear R on FP to cross another stile. Continue ahead keeping the hedge on R until path exits onto North Standen Road. Turn R and follow road to cross the High Street diagonally L and take a passage way to the R of the bridge back to the station.

② **Short Walk -**Leave car park by footpath to the High Street. Cross road, turn R and take FP opposite Post Office. Continue to reach St. Laurence's Church. Turn L uphill to reach Smitham Bridge Road and turn R. Just after road turns R take FP on L opposite Marsh Lane. Continue to end of path and take stile in far R corner, through small woodland, to cross another stile. At field turn L on well defined path to a sign that advises you the rest of the path is now private. Cross stile on L and follow FP across middle of field to stile by main gate of Standen Manor. Turn L on road and continue ahead to meet the A338. Cross this to the L and take the FP to join the Inkpen Road at Hornhill. Turn L along road and at Sanham Green turn L on FP between farm buildings which soon bears R, crosses a FP and exits on Priory Road. Turn L then take a small FP opposite Our Lady of Lourdes church to take you to the High Street. Follow this back to the station.

St. Laurences Church, Hungerford

Walk 4

Little Common

Start - Hungerford Station.

Parking - Station Rd. car park (pay & display) or Hungerford Common.

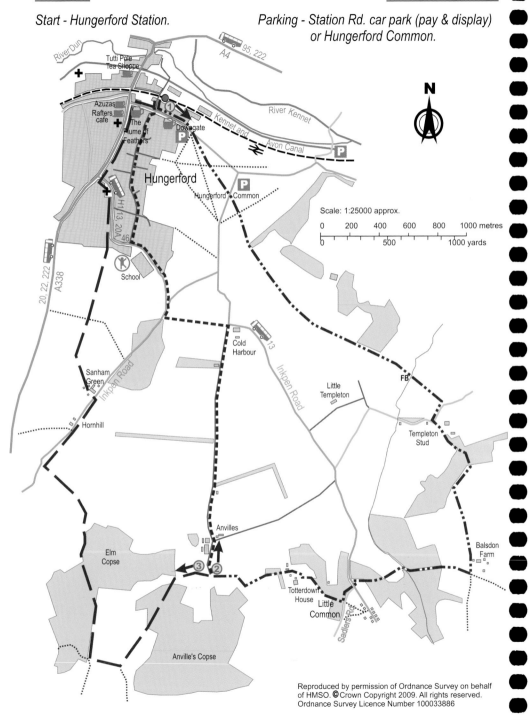

Scale: 1:25000 approx.

0   200   400   600   800   1000 metres
0   500   1000 yards

① Leave station car park by vehicular entrance, turn R and at next road turn L towards Hungerford Common. At Downgate Pub use pedestrian entrance to common taking direction shown on map, aiming for R side of distant trees. At trees cross road at FP sign and take path diagonally R across field to gate. Through gate turn sharp L and follow field edge path to cross FB and reach a road. Turn R for about 100m then L into estate. Just after telephone pole on R turn R on FP between fences to go through gate and turn R. Follow this path until it turns L. At stud continue ahead following the beech hedge then when road on L turns L turn R between beech hedges into woodland. Cross FB and follow path to more woodland. At Inkpen

From Anvilles South to Wayfarer's Walk

Short walk para. 2   Long walk para.3

② At the gate turn R and follow the FP keeping the farm buildings on your R to meet a road on a bend. Take the FP on the L to meet another road and turn R then take the L fork into Priory Road. Beyond the school turn R into Priory Avenue and follow this back to the station car park.

③ Go through the gate on path going diagonally L. After 50m turn sharp L through wood then cross a field heading for large oak tree in the distance on the R. At oak tree continue towards a stile, **do not cross stile**. Turn R to go through a gate at R corner of field. Turn sharp R and follow path to the end of the wood where the path turns L towards Inkpen Road. Turn R on road to Sanham Green then turn L on FP between farm buildings then bear R with the path. When FP joins Priory Road turn L on Priory Rd. then R on FP opposite the church and follow to the High Street. Continue down High St. and follow signs back to the station.

The Path to Totterdown House

Rd. cross L into Sadlers Rd. for about 50m then turn R on paved road. Just before Totterdown House take FP on R to go through 2 gates, cross a stile and continue across a field to another gate. Continue this direction across an open area to a gate where there are 3 FP signs.

Shepherd's Bridge

Walk 5

Start - Kintbury Station
Parking - British Waterways free Car park.

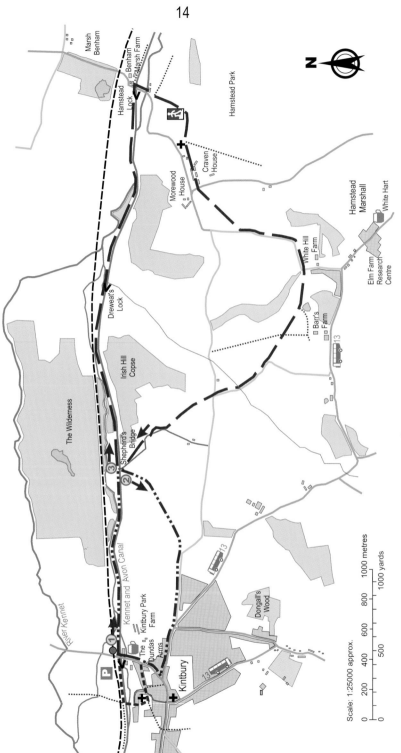

Scale: 1:25000 approx.

| 0 | 200 | 400 | 600 | 800 | 1000 metres |

| 0 | | 500 | | | 1000 yards |

Walk 5 Shepherd's Bridge

Short route 2.5 miles (4km)   Long route 6 miles (9.5km)

① Park at public car park by the canal, walk onto the canal towpath, turn L to cross the road and continue to the first bridge, Shepherds Bridge. For the long walk continue on towpath, for the short walk cross the bridge and take the FP on the R.

Short walk - para 2   Long walk - para 3

cross to L and enter churchyard through gate. Turn R on FP passing to L of church and follow this across the canal bridge to turn R on towpath back to the car park.

opposite then diagonally L across field heading for the middle of 3 oak trees to join a track. Continue ahead to shortly go through a gate on R, turn sharp L and go diagonally R across a field to Shepherds Bridge.

Do not cross the bridge but take the FP on the L, *(shown as ② on the map)*. Follow FP diagonally R, uphill, until it joins a tarmac track. Continue ahead on the track to a gate onto a road. Turn R on road to a junction and turn R again. At T junction turn R, cross to pavement opposite and follow back to the car park.

The Kennet & Avon Canal at Kintbury

Shepherds Bridge

② Follow FP diagonally R, uphill, until it joins a tarmac track. Continue ahead on the track to a gate onto a road. Turn R on road to a junction and turn R again. At T junction turn R, cross to pavement opposite and after about 180m take the FP L. At road

③ Continue on the towpath for about 1.5 miles to Hamstead lock, (No. 81). Turn R across the bridge and as the road bends R turn L through a gate to enter Hampstead Park. Almost immediately turn R on FP uphill to bear R behind the church and pass through 2 huge gate posts on to a gravel road between houses. At the road junction cross the road and a stile opposite. At next stile cross the field diagonally to the far L corner, cross a FB to a gate onto a road. Turn L onto road until it turns sharp L just beyond Whitehill Farm then turn R on FP going diagonally L across field between 2 oak trees. At track turn L and almost immediately R through a squeeze gate, continuing ahead through 2 more squeeze gates to reach a stile at road. Turn R and follow road to T junction, cross the stile

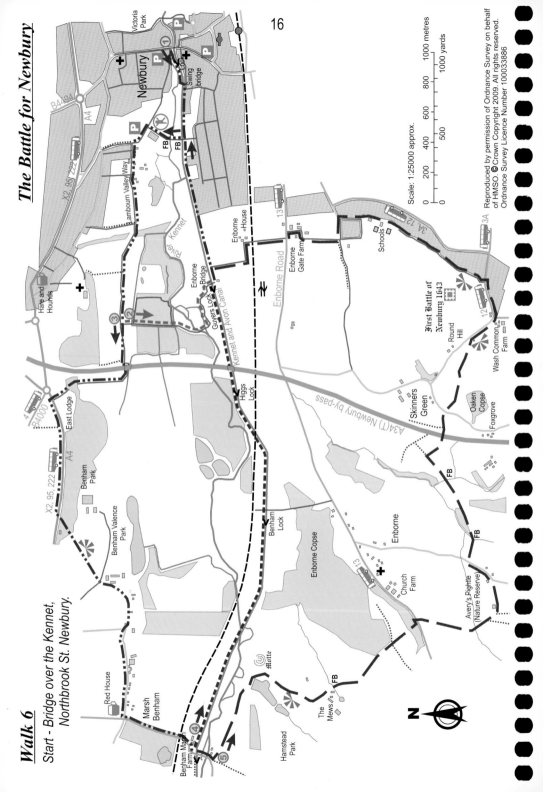

The Battle for Newbury

Walk 6

Start - Bridge over the Kennet, Northbrook St. Newbury.

16

Scale: 1:25000 approx.

Reproduced by permission of Ordnance Survey on behalf of HMSO. © Crown Copyright 2009. All rights reserved. Ordnance Survey Licence Number 100033886

Walk 6   The Battle for Newbury

Start - Bridge over the Kennet, Northbrook St., Newbury

Short 3 miles (5km)   Medium 7 miles (11km)
Long 9.5 miles (15km)

① Go down alley way between Clarks and Holland and Barrett. Follow path L through tunnel, over FB and along to swing bridge. Cross bridge and turn R. Go along towpath and turn R over first bridge. Follow path to road. Turn L past leisure centre, follow path around to R. Turn L to follow a broad, unmade road signed 'Lambourn Valley Way'. Go under the old railway bridge and straight ahead on FP to second metal kissing gate.

Short route para 2, Medium/Long para 3

② *(Shown light green)*. Go through the gate and turn L onto 'permitted path'. Follow path as it curves around to reach the canal. Go over bridge, turn L and return to start.

③ Continue ahead from gate and follow around to L to go under A34 road bridge then R, uphill, to reach main A4. Cross over and turn L on pavement. After about 750m cross back over road to small wooden gate in wall. Go through gate to follow path through wood and maintain direction down hill and round to R through gate posts to public road. Follow road around to L, past estate cottages, to crossroads. Turn L to go over railway and reach canal.

Medium route - para4 Long route - para 5

④ Turn L onto canal towpath and follow this back to the start point.

Narrow boat at Marsh Benham

⑤ Follow road over canal and 50m after Hamstead Mill turn L into Hamstead Park. Follow tarmac path over bridge and around to R. At cattle grid by houses turn L and continue ahead. Where hedge turns R continue diagonally R to reach drive. Turn L and follow drive. At junction of paths continue ahead to road. Cross diagonally L and follow FP bearing R to corner of field. Continue ahead over 2 stiles then bear L and continue ahead with hedge on R. Cross stile and take path to L. At open field keep hedge on L to reach road. Turn L along road and take FP on R. At open field go ahead to bridge then bear slightly L towards 2 large trees and at small bridge turn R. Go over A34 road bridge and continue ahead to cross lane. Go ahead on field path to cross stile on L and continue uphill with hedge on L. Where hedge ends maintain direction up hill and at top exit L to lane. Turn R and at main road cross over and turn L on pavement. Take path on L opposite Battle Road. At bottom of hill bear L keeping both schools on your L and follow alleyway ahead. At road turn R and at T-junction turn L. At junction of FPs turn R. At road cross over and turn L and then R along track to reach canal. Turn R on towpath to return to start.

Walk 7
Start - Donnington Castle Car Park

Donnington Castle

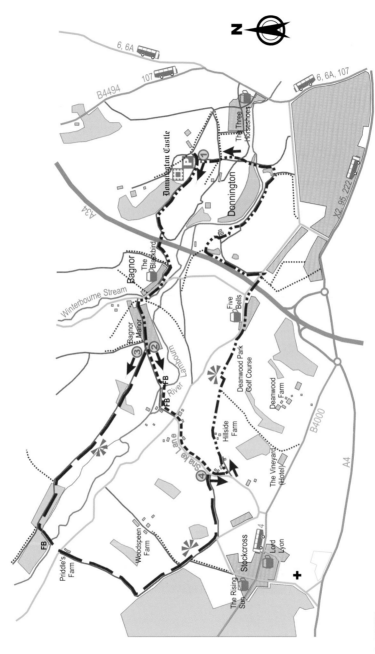

Scale: 1:25000 approx.

Walk 7 Donnington Castle

Short 3.75 miles (6km)   Long 6 miles (9.5km)

① Go to the end of the car park and go straight ahead to follow the R hand path. At junction turn L and follow path through tunnel of bushes. Go over road bridge, follow L around and at bottom go through gate and turn R to pass Blackbird pub. Take second turning L to pass the manor house gates, go over stile on R of the large wooden gates and reach a fork in the path.

Short walk-para 2   Long walk-para 3

② Go over the stile and follow the path between 2 fences. Follow FP over bridges bear L along drive, cross the road and go ahead up the lane to where the byway (from the long walk) joins from the R.

Go to paragraph 4

③ Take the wide track to the R for 3/4 mile (1.3km). Take the signed FP to the L over the bridge to the road. Cross road and continue on track opposite as it turns L to reach a road on a sharp corner. Go L ahead for 20m then take the track (byway)

Donnington Castle

on the L to meet another road. Turn R.

Go to paragraph 4

④ Follow road for 160m and, at a FP sign, turn L along a gravel drive. At 'Hillside' continue ahead to go through a gate and maintain direction alongside a wooden fence. At the corner turn R to cross a stile. Cross field diagonally to reach a fence. Follow fence to R up hill to reach a stile in the hedge. Go over both stiles, turn R and follow field edge. At the end of the field cross stile on L to reach the road. Pass the Five Bells pub and use pavement on R to pass under the bridge then take the first turning L (signed 'Golf Course Maintenance Dept'.) Where this road turns R continue ahead along a FP next to wire fence. Turn R onto FP and cross a small service road then a bridge to reach a drive. Turn L and go over the bridges, take the R fork and continue on the grass beside the drive. Where the drive turns L take the signed FP straight ahead and follow this back to the start.

Walk 8

Start - Snelsmore Common Car Park

Snelsmore Common

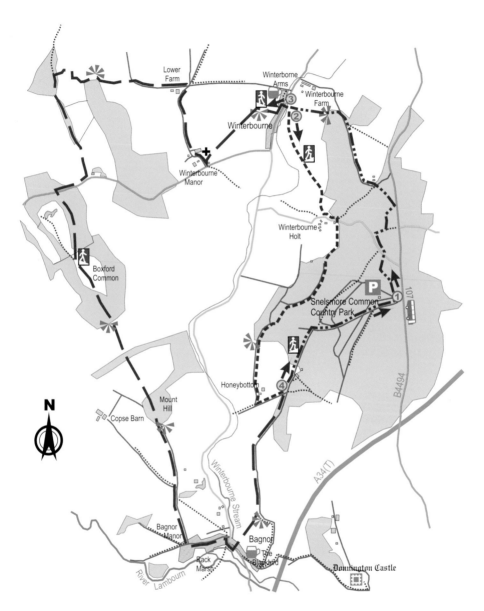

Scale: 1:25000 approx.

0   200   400   600   800   1000 metres

0   500   1000 yards

① From the car park nearest the road take the permitted bridleway to the R of the overhead barrier. Follow this as it winds to the lane. Turn L along the lane and R on to restricted byway. At junction take L fork, signed, 'Permitted Bridleway' to road. Turn L on to broad track and at house bear L on signed bridleway with wire fence on R. Turn L on FP and at field turn L for 15m then R to reach the edge of Winterbourne village.

Short route - para. 2   Long route - para. 3

② Just before the FB turn L along path heading uphill across field. Go over stile and continue ahead. At next stile go diagonally L to corner of field, through gate and along field edge with fence on L. At next gate continue along field edge to lane. Turn L. At end of property turn R on to FP. Follow this with wall, then fence on R for about half a mile, (0.8km). Go through wooden gate and follow path around to L. At open field go ahead keeping hedge on L. Go through gate and along drive. Turn L and at junction of tracks turn L. Continue to gate at edge of Snelsmore Common.

Go to paragraph 4.

③ Cross FB to road. Turn L then R at Summer Cottage. Follow field edge path. At open field continue ahead under power line to church. Go around L side of church and through small, wooden gate. Turn R on broad track past farm buildings then continue ahead. At Lower Farm turn L at bridleway junction with fence/hedge first on L, then on R. After short section of wood turn L along field edge and through gate on L. Turn R and follow field edge to large,

metal field gate. **Do not go through gate.** Continue to follow field edge keeping fence on R, go through 3 kissing gates to reach road. Turn R uphill, then turn L on to FP. Follow signs through wood. Go over stile and turn half L to reach second stile. Continue ahead to reach another stile at far end of Boxford Common. Follow path through short wood, keep hedge on L to go through small copse and follow signs to eventually reach junction of bridleways at back of Bagnor Manor. Turn L passing ornamental gates. Continue along lane to road. Turn R and, just past Brook House, turn L on FP. At top of hill turn L on to bridle way. Follow this to reach gate on edge of Snelsmore Common.

Go to paragraph 4

Winterbourne Stream

④ Go through gate and ahead on bridle way. At top of hill turn R on broad track and follow bridleway signs back to car park.

Walk 9

Historic Newbury

Start - Bridge over the Kennet, Northbrook St.

Scale: 1:25000 approx.

```
0     200    400    600    800    1000 metres
0              500            1000 yards
```

① From the old stone bridge over the River Kennet in the centre of Newbury walk up Northbrook St. and turn R between Costa Coffee and West Cornwall Pasty Co. Continue along the towpath. Just past the bridge turn L and follow the avenue of trees through the park. Go ahead into Park Lane and at the main road turn L to the pedestrian crossing. Cross over into Hawthorn Road, turn R into Chestnut Crescent and at the first turning go R to the dual carriage way. Turn R to go through the underpass, up the steps and along the path to reach the park.

Short walk-para. 2   Long walk-para. 3

② Cross the bridge over the stream and turn L. At the end of the park turn L through the underpass. Turn R past the playground and go over the bridge. Turn L through the housing estate and R at the pillar box to reach the main road. Turn L and cross over just past the school to go along the path beside the road. At the junction turn R and just past The Castle pub cross the road to follow the FP across the cricket ground. Turn R at the fence, go behind the pavilion, at the gate turn on to the road.

Go to para. 4

③ Continue ahead through the park. At the road turn L and continue past the church and school to the T junction. Cross the road and take the R hand FP around the Vodaphone complex. At the roundabout continue on the R hand pavement and turn R onto the footpath. Continue under the tunnel, over the stile and along the path to the road. Cross the road and turn L past the hotel entrance. Turn R at the FP and follow it through the car parks and over the bridge. Turn L, follow the FP to the junction of paths, turn L and maintain direction across the track to follow the path to the road.

Go to para. 4

④ Turn R along the private road to the car park of Donnington Castle. Turn L and go to the end of the car park, turn L and follow the path to the tarmac drive. Bearing L go along the drive, over the bridges and at the FP turn R. After 20m turn L along the FP to the gate ignoring the 2 tarmac paths. Do not go through the gate. Turn R for about 250 metres to go through a gate on L. Turn R in Grove Road   then carefully cross into Station Road to follow this to the main A4.

The Ladywell

Turn L for about 30m and cross to go up steps into an alley way to a road. Turn R then L onto a FP just past Ladywell House. Go through the churchyard, turn L then R onto a FP and follow to a junction of paths. Turn L and follow FP which becomes a track just before railway bridge. Follow track to reach park. Turn R then just past the leisure centre turn R on FP over the canal bridge. Turn L and follow the tow path to the swing bridge just past Kennet Road. Cross the bridge, turn R and follow path back to start.

Three Commons

Walk 10

Start - Greenham Common Car Park, (at junction of Bury's Bank Road & Greenham Road).

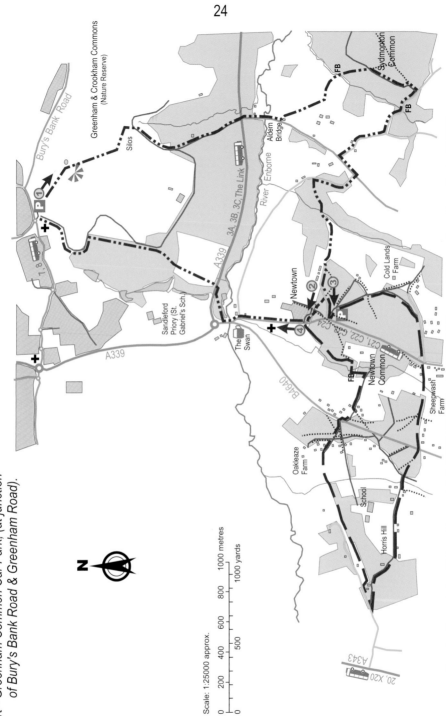

Scale: 1:25000 approx.

0	200	400	600	800	1000 metres
0		500			1000 yards

① From car park go through gate on L of green, wire gates. Go straight ahead. At pond follow the diagonal path to wire fence, turn L and at corner turn R. At lane turn L and on reaching main A339 road, **taking great care**, go straight across. Follow road signed, 'Burghclere Schools' and take first FP on L. Go diagonally R across field and go through gap in hedge. Turn L and follow field edge around to R. Turn L at path sign and go down to bridge. Go upwards through wood, bear R onto straight path. At junction turn R to reach road. Turn R and at road junction turn R. At main road turn L then take first R. Turn L on first FP across field and follow through wood to cross footbridge. Turn L then bear R to go along field edge. Go through gap on R towards houses and along lane.

Short route - para 2   Long route - para 3

② Take path on R 130m after houses. Bear L alongside green fencing, turn R and follow sign to reach village hall. Take FP on L to reach road. Turn R.

Go to paragraph 4.

③ Continue on lane into car park on L by road. Take main track through extra parking area and bear R past metal barrier. Go straight on noting horse shoes on trees. Follow path under power lines to join drive on L when gap appears. Turn R to cross road. Continue ahead to cross second road (B4640). Go ahead and take FP on R by power line support cables. At bottom of hill go ahead at junction and follow path through playing fields then through woods. At lane turn sharp R. Go over stile on R to continue to corner of field. Go ahead on edge of wood, then along field edge over stiles, 2 streams and past houses. Turn L at tarmac drive to reach main road. Cross diagonally R and follow path around to L. Take path ahead and follow to cross stream. Just after L bend follow path to L keeping low bank on L. At road turn L.

Go to paragraph 4

④ Go down road past church and at pub bear L to reach main road. Turn R and go down steps on R. Go diagonally L across field to meet main A339 road. **Take great care** to cross road diagonally R and take track on L. Follow FP across field. Follow broad path ahead through wood and then follow yellow waymark signs back to start.

Silos at Greenham Common

Stream on Newtown Common

Walk 11

The Reed Beds

Start: Thatcham Nature Discovery Centre
(Link to station 1 mile via towpath)

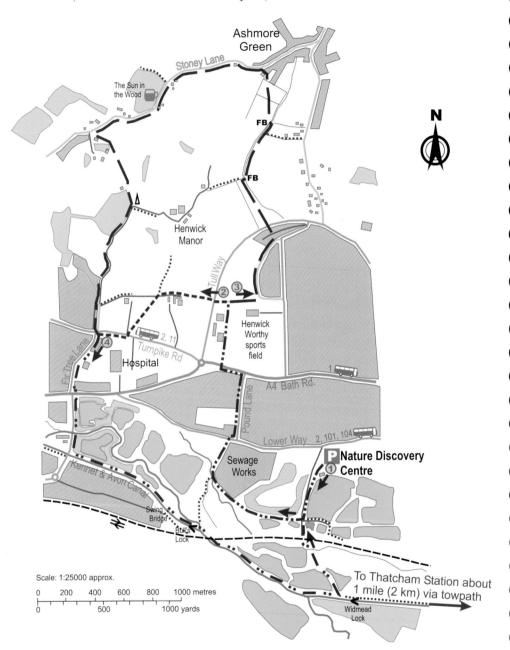

Scale: 1:25000 approx.

① From the Discovery Centre walk down the R side of the lake to a junction of tracks. Take centre broad track. As this bends L at sign keep right to walk around the edge of the sewage works to reach Lower Way. Turn R then L up Pound Lane to the A4 and turn L. Use the road islands to cross the A4 and go up the FP between the garden centre and the playing field to the top.

Short route para. 2 - Long route para. 3

View across Newbury from Henwick

② Turn L to follow the FP. Cross Tull Way to FP opposite and pass buildings on the L to reach a stile on the L at the corner of a field. Cross the stile and go diagonally across the field to another stile and cross Turnpike Rd. Turn R to the road junction.

Continue at para. 4

③ Turn R to end of FP then L to walk down a road. After first 2 houses on L turn L down a FP to cross a small Rd. and Tull Way into a long field. At almost the end of this field turn R over a stile and FB then turn L along field edge to cross another stile. Keep stream on L to turn L over a FB & stile then half R across a field to a 2nd stile. Continue to a 3rd stile. Bear slightly L to go through a gate by a bungalow, up the drive and over another stile onto Stony Lane. Turn L for about 1/2 mile (1km) until, just before a row of houses on the L, turn L on to a FP. Pass a flat roofed house on R and cross a stile. Bear half R to follow a path to a phone mast and bear R down a track to cross an estate road and continue to meet Turnpike Rd. Cross to the junction with Fir Tree Lane.

Continue at para. 4

④ Turn L down Fir Tree Lane and use the crossing lights carefully to cross the busy A4 and continue down Hambridge Rd. crossing the River Kennet at Ham Bridge. By a low wall bear left to join the canal towpath. Follow this past Bull's Lock and under the railway until, just before Widmead Lock, turn L over a stile on a FP between the lakes. Cross the railway line with great care and follow the path back to the Discovery Centre.

Confluence of Canal & River at Bull's Lock

Walk 12

Start: Bradley Moore Square

The Two Pubs

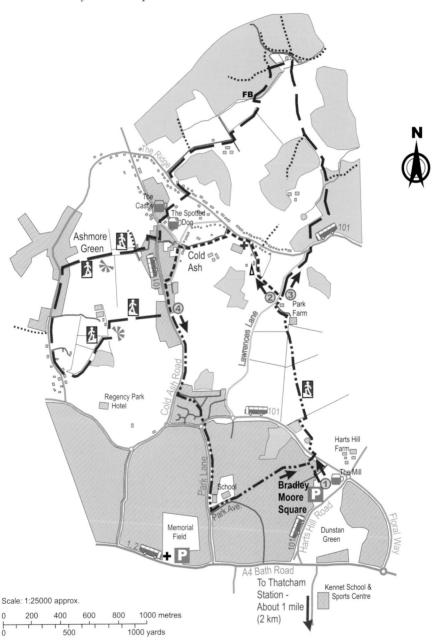

N

The Ridge

FB

The Castle

The Spotted Dog

Ashmore Green

Cold Ash

101

④

② ③ Park Farm

Lawrences Lane

Cold Ash Road

Regency Park Hotel

Park Lane

School

101

Harts Hill Farm

The Mill

①

P

Bradley Moore Square

Park Ave.

Harts Hill Road

Floral Way

Memorial Field

1, 2

101

+ P

Dunstan Green

A4 Bath Road

To Thatcham Station - About 1 mile (2 km)

Kennet School & Sports Centre

Scale: 1:25000 approx.

0   200   400   600   800   1000 metres

0   500   1000 yards

① With shops on your L leave car park across play area, cross Foxglove Way and go into Cowslip Crescent. At mini roundabout turn R on FP to cross Floral Way, over stile and onto field path. Bear R around pond then follow field edge uphill to hedge, turn R for 60m then L over stile through hedge. Continue ahead uphill to cross second stile heading towards farm. Look for third stile in hedge on L and cross this to bear R and head for fourth stile in the fence at side of farm drive. Cross this and turn L to meet Lawrences Lane. Turn R and walk about 50m to see a metal gate up on the L.

Short walk para. 2   Long walk para. 3

② Pass through gate and cross field to go through similar gate by aerial and follow path round to R and down track to road. Turn L past convent and house and take first turning L down a small road, turning R before the end down a track behind the houses to meet Collaroy Road. Turn L and follow this to meet Cold Ash Road. Cross road, turn L downhill to pass the last house on L where the long walk route joins from R.

Go to paragraph 4

③ Continue up Lawrences Lane to the top. Cross road, turn R and at wood edge turn L on FP downhill into wood. At fence bear R to follow FP, straight on at pine trees, across 2 ditches then turning L across another ditch and uphill following edge of wood on L. Where FP forks take L path and follow to clearing with houses L & R. Turn L through old gate with house on R and follow FP into wood. At crossing path turn L on FP curving around to R and at FP sign turn L over 2 FBs and gate into field. Turn L, through gap in hedge ahead, then R with hedge on R to go through gate and continue uphill, along field edge to another gate. Go through gate, turn L for 30m then R on track past house on L and uphill to The Ridge. Turn L for 200m then R at signed FP to emerge by 2 pubs onto Cold Ash Road. Cross road to pavement, turn L down hill for about 120m then R into Spring Lane. Follow this track between houses to 2 stiles and cross these to follow field edge uphill over second stile then cross a third stile on L and follow narrow path downhill with fence on L to meet Ashmore Green Road and turn L. Follow road past houses and long hedge to a FP sign on R. Turn L up short drive to stile then follow FP with fence on L and copse on R, over stile, uphill, through kissing gate, turn L along field edge then R on mid field path downhill to road. Turn R.

Go to paragraph 4

④ Go down the road, crossing where the pavement runs out, to where the houses on the L restart and take first L, Southend, then first R, to follow path between hedges to Floral Way. Cross the road, go R then L down Park Lane, past the old school and L into Park Avenue. Just past Thatcham Park School bear L onto a FP and follow this across a road to the end. Cross Foxglove Way and continue ahead to follow Cowslip Crescent around to the R, back to the start.

Walk 13

Start: Bradley Moor Square

Above the Kennet Valley

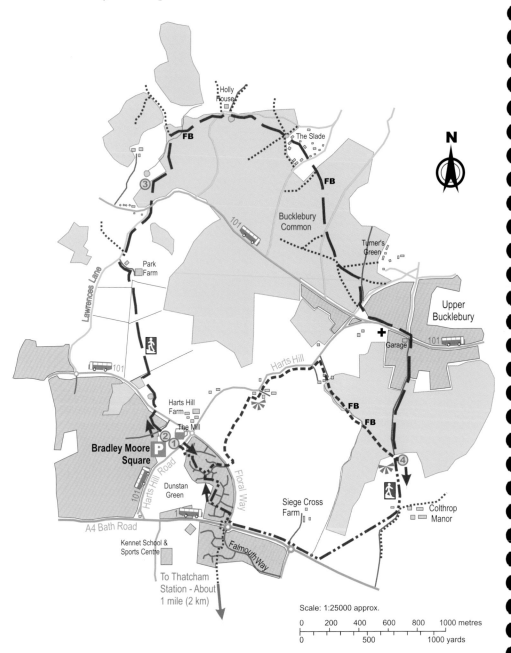

Scale: 1:25000 approx.

① *Short Walk* - Cross Harts Hill Rd. at the crossing point and go ahead on urban FP to the end. Turn L to follow Simmons Field Rd. and cross Floral Way. Follow the permitted path uphill past the white house then up some steps to continue alongside Harts Hill. At the second track turn R. Just past the house cross the stile on the L and the fence then bear R to cross stile and FB in bottom R corner. Bear R up the bank and follow the field edge to corner. Enter wood over FB, turn R then L and follow clear FP through the woods to a gate at the wood edge. Turn R.

Continue at paragraph 4

② *Long Walk* - With shops on your L leave car park across play area, cross Foxglove Way and go into Cowslip Crescent. At mini roundabout turn R on FP to cross Floral Way, over stile and onto field path. Bear R around pond then follow field edge uphill to hedge, turn R for 60m then L over stile through hedge. Continue ahead uphill to cross second stile heading towards farm. Look for third stile in hedge/fence on L and cross this to bear R and head for fourth stile in fence at side of farm drive. Cross this and turn L to meet Lawrences Lane, turn R and continue to the top. Cross road, turn R and at wood edge turn L on FP downhill into wood.

③ At fence bear R to follow FP straight on at pine trees, across 2 ditches then turning L across another ditch and uphill following edge of wood on L. Where FP forks take R fork, bear L over FB and keep bank on left to meet a road. Turn L, pass Holly House on L and just past 2 low culvert walls bear R at bridleway sign to follow faint path uphill bearing L to emerge on open green at junction of 5 paths. Pass to R of small pond and take FP next to house, through The Slade to cross a road onto Bucklebury Common. Follow FP down, over FB and uphill following waymarks to cross a road. Take the bridleway path bearing L onto byway at waymark and follow this to turn R on to gravel track, R then L at minor road and, at Bucklebury, turn L through the village. Turn R down track by garage and follow this into and through woods to emerge on field path overlooking Colthrop.

Continue at paragraph 4

Across the Kennet Valley to Hampshire

④ Follow path to pass through gate at Colthrop Manor then bear R at signpost on FP across field, over stile and across next field to gate in far corner. Turn R along A4 then R into Floral Way. By the post box turn L onto urban FP into Poppy Drive then R following FP into Broadmeadow End, L along FP then R at end through Pimpernel Place to pick up FP again on R back to Bradley Moore Square.

Walk 14   *Greenham Common*

Start: Thatcham Nature Discovery Centre
     (Or Thatcham Station joining routes at points 2 or 3)

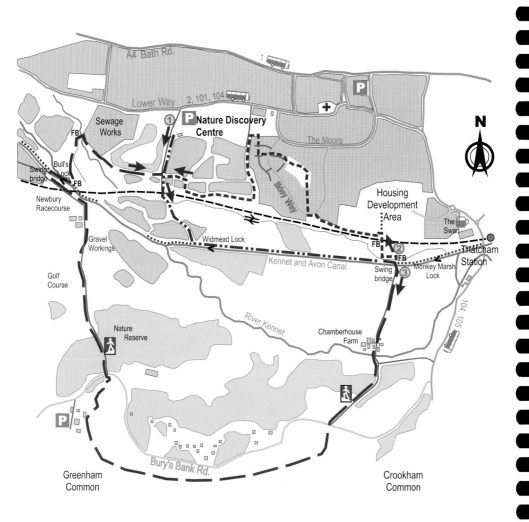

① Walk away from the Discovery Center with the lake on your L to follow the track to the railway. Carefully cross the line and continue on the path between the lakes to the canal. Turn L and follow the towpath to the swing bridge.

Short route para. 2 - Long route para. 3

The Swing Bridge

②Turn L away from the canal across a FB and follow the path to cross the railway over a FB turning sharp L at the bottom to follow FP with railway on L. As bank on R ends, take path ahead between metal fenced compounds to open grassy area. Bear R with garden fences on R to reach Ilkley Way. Cross road, turn L for 50 m then turn R down urban FP. At open area keep ahead then take path on L around edge of area to first house on L. Here go ahead through Tadham Place to cross Ilkley Way and go L then R into short FP. At end go through close to take FP on R and continue to playing field. Turn immediately L across grass then L again at gravel track. Follow this through a car park and around lakes on R as shown on map. At gravel track turn L then at crossing track turn R back to start.

③ Turn R across the swing bridge and follow the track through the farm, across the river, R at junction and uphill to cross Burys Bank Rd. Go through the gate onto the common, turn R and pick a route across the common towards the old control tower. As the control tower appears bear R on a path towards a large, brown building. Just before this bear R on FP through a metal gate and after about 60m, just before a yellow ringed marker post, go L on a faint path towards trees. Turn L through gap in brambles and keep fence on L to go through a gate. Carefully cross the road onto FP downhill to cross a stile by houses, go under railway bridge and turn R over a swing bridge. Turn R again onto towpath, cross a FB over the river then turn sharp L and bear R away from the river on a FP through reed beds. Cross a FB by a notice board, turn R and, keeping the fence on your L, go ahead crossing a metal bridge and bearing L at a broad track, back to the start.

The Old Control Tower

Walk 15 — Between Two Rivers

Start: Thatcham Railway Station - (Parking Pay & Display.
Alternative parking at Burdwood Centre)

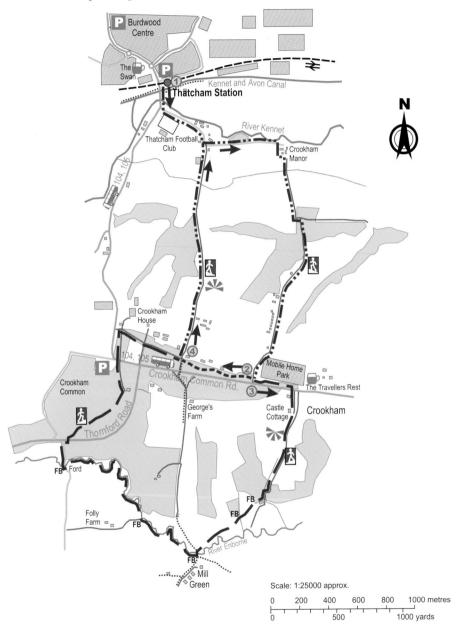

Scale: 1:25000 approx.

0 200 400 600 800 1000 metres
0 500 1000 yards

① From the station cross the canal and river bridges and turn L into Chamberhouse Mill Road. Follow this as it becomes a gravel track and at a large white house (Crookham Willows) turn L. Just before Crookham Manor turn R at fence and follow path around the house to turn R past tennis court. Pass through a gate and follow the field edge path into wood, bending L then almost immediately turning R at sign. Follow path uphill to join a concrete, then tarmac road to Crookham Common Road.

Short walk para. 2   Long walk para. 3

② Turn R on a narrow but distinct path through the trees, parallel to the road, crossing two tracks, a green and a drive to reach a tarmac, crossing road. Turn Right.

Go to paragraph. 4

③ Turn L to follow a sometimes overgrown FP on the L (or the road), to see a bungalow on the R. Turn R through wrought iron gates with brick pillars,(Castle Cottage), and continue down the drive, past the house and downhill to turn R at the wood edge. Bear L with the track then turn R passing to the rear of the building now on your L, (currently a ruin). Cross a FB and maintain direction across the field ahead to a 2nd FB then diagonally L across the next field heading well L of the mid-field telegraph pole. Join the riverside track and turn R to reach a FB. Cross the bridge, turn sharp R to cross a stile then R to follow the winding, riverside FP. Cross another stile to a road by a ford. Turn R to cross the river on the FB and go uphill to Thornford Road. Turn R for about 20m then cross road to a faint path which bends R then L up a gully. At the top maintain direction ahead through a dell to bear R on a broad path which bends L, goes through a gate and bears L to Crookham Common Road. Cross road and go down track opposite to turn R at crossing track. Go over the first gravel crossing track then at the tarmac road turn L.

Go to paragraph. 4

Weir on the Enborne river

④ Follow the road straight on, through a gate on to a track and continue downhill to join Chamberhouse Mill Road and back to the start.

Walk 16

Douai Abbey

*Start - Row Barge PH car park. (20 spaces for public use)
or Midgham Station.*

Scale: 1:25000 approx.

| 0 | 200 | 400 | 600 | 800 | 1000 metres |

| 0 | | 500 | | 1000 yards |

① Turn L out of car park and follow Station Road over canal and railway to the A4. Cross at lights then turn R to garage and petrol station to take FP on L between the two, climbing to reach road. Turn R and, opposite Elstree School, take FP on L. Follow this to go L through wood, then R up field edge to enter wood ahead. At junction of FPs turn R in wood then L up field edge turning R at top on to road at Kiff Green. Turn R along road and, just past Kiff Green Farm, take FP on R diagonally across paddock to rejoin road; (if muddy stay on road). Cross road, over stile, turn R and follow inside field margin to gravel track. Turn L to reach entrance to wood at junction of paths.

Short walk - para 2   Long walk - para 3

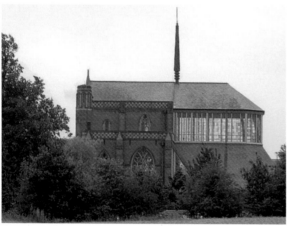

Douai Abbey

② Turn sharp R across field towards Douai Abbey. Follow path over road to cul de sac to reach road at Abbey Gardens and cross to tarmac path between tennis courts and road, (avoiding narrow lane). At road turn L past schools and church to turn L on FP at top of hill and retrace outward route to A4 and start point.

③ Turn L along field edge then R along wood edge to reach electricity substation. Turn L through wood to reach field and turn L then R along field edges, only crossing into second field on L near bottom of slope. Turn R across stream, take track to R and, just after Pogles Wood Cottage, take FP on L to recreation ground and Blade Bone PH. Turn L towards Upper Bucklebury and Thatcham and, just past sign to 'Scotland Corner' on R, take byway on L. Just after Spring Cottage go ahead away from road on R, go L at cross track then R on byway about 100m before house. At next cross track turn L towards house then R on byway near sign, 'Carbins Wood' and, where byway bends R after 2 houses, turn L, initially following line of overhead cables, to reach an area of open common with bridleway going off to R. Take byway to L and, shortly before Carbinswood Lane, take track on R to avoid very wet area ahead. Turn L on road then ahead on FP to Midgham, passing to R of 'Woottens' and on to road. Turn R along road and, just after junction with Birds Lane, take FP on L through garden of West Lodge, next to Midgham Church, crossing Midgham Park to reach road at East Lodge. Turn R down hill to A4, turn L and, opposite Falmouth Arms, take FP on R. Follow around to Station Road and turn R back to start.

Walk 17

The Wolf Walk

Start - Aldermaston Wharf Visitor Centre, (free parking). (A short walk from Aldermaston Station)

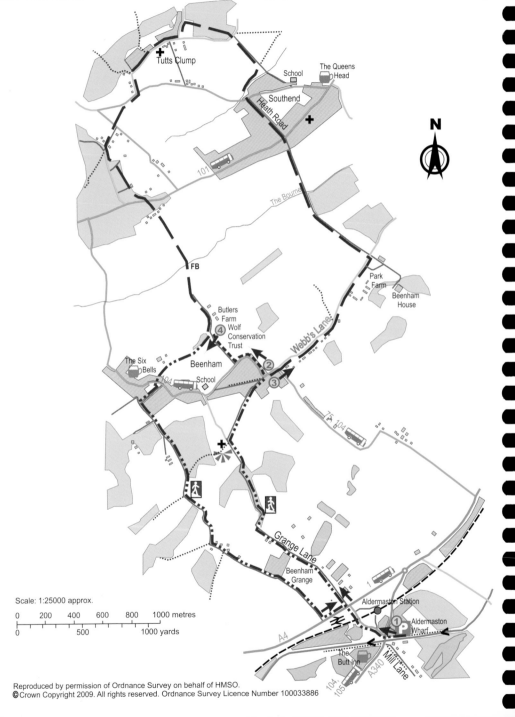

Scale: 1:25000 approx.

0   200   400   600   800   1000 metres

0   500   1000 yards

Walk 17 The Wolf Walk
Short 3.5 miles (5.5km) Long 7 miles (11km)

① From car park turn R onto towpath. Cross A340, go along Station Road past station entrances, over bridge and cross A4 to enter Grange Lane towards Beenham industrial area. Bear R at large cedar tree at the green and continue up track, past Wayside Cottage to reach Beenham Church. Take FP on R opposite church gate to reach road and main road at a bend.

Para 2 - short route   Para 3 - long route

Beenham Church

② Turn L along road, past garage and around bend to reach FP at a drive on R. Walk down drive to reach entrance to UK Wolf Conservation Trust and take FP on L, into trees to join the long route.

Go to paragraph 4

③ Continue along road to mini roundabout at sharp bend then go ahead along Webb's Lane. 75m past Beenham House on R, take bridleway on L across fields and through copse to reach road at Bradfield Southend. Cross into Heath Road and at far end take FP to L of house, 'Holly Tree', on other side of lane, following it around behind houses, then edge of field. Exit field and turn L along bridleway at 2 squeeze stiles to reach road at house, 'Cherry Orchard'. Enter FP into wood opposite, passing under bridge on sunken section, to reach another road at top of hill between Tutts Clump and Rotten Row. Turn L along road, R at road junction to pass through Tutts Clump, and around L bend to reach another junction near an underground reservoir. Turn R for 100m to take FP on L through kissing gate and go diagonally R across field to reach road. Take FP to R of Glenvale Nurseries and, on reaching the common near house, turn L on byway, bearing R at house, 'Smithincott'. After 50m leave track and take FP on L, crossing 2 gravel drives to reach main road at avenue of oak trees. Cross road, turn L, almost immediately taking drive on R and at division in track take FP on L following it down into field and heading for bottom hedge just to L of electricity pole. Cross FB into second field and go diagonally R towards trees. Cross stile and follow edge of next 2 fields to reach Butler's Farm, following drive up to entrance to UK Wolf Conservation Trust. Where drive bears L take FP ahead into trees .

Go to paragraph 4

④ Cross stile into field, turn R along field edge, over stile into second field and head towards garden shed and narrow FP on to road opposite recreation ground. Turn L along road then R along far edge of recreation ground and between houses to reach cross track. Turn L to follow track, at first on the level, then downhill to reach the A4. Turn L along road and at Grange Lane go R, across the A4, into Station Road and back to start.

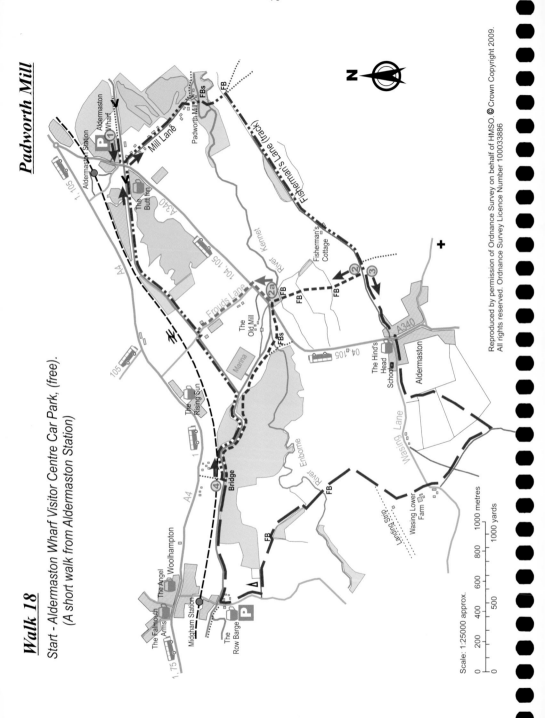

Walk 18

Start - Aldermaston Wharf Visitor Centre Car Park, (free).
(A short walk from Aldermaston Station)

Padworth Mill

Aldermaston Station
Aldermaston Wharf
Mill Lane
Padworth Mill
FBs
FB
Fisherman's Lane (track)
The Butt Inn
A340
Kennet
River
Fisherman's Cottage
FB
FB
Frouds Lane
The Old Mill
FBs
The Hind's Head School
A340
Aldermaston
Wasing Lane
Manor
The Rising Sun
River Enborne
Wasing Lower Farm
Landing Strip
Bridge
FB
FB
The Angel
Woolhampton
A4
The Falmouth Arms
Midgham Station
The Row Barge

N

Scale: 1:25000 approx.

0   200   400   600   800   1000 metres

0   500   1000 yards

① From car park turn R onto towpath. Go over the canal bridge and turn L into Mill Lane, (signed Alder Bridge School). Just before Padworth Mill turn R on signed narrow, fenced FP, following this over weirs and across field beyond. At end of field cross FB and turn R along field edge. At second metal kissing gate go onto Fisherman's Lane. Follow this until, about 400m after Fisherman's Cottage, you reach gate and FP on R.

Short route - para 2   Long route - para 3

② Turn R to cross 2 fields, enter a copse and reach main Basingstoke road. ②ⓐ [*To shorten your walk to 3 miles turn R across bridge then L into Frouds Lane to reach bridge over canal, (this route is shown in light green), then turn R along towpath back to start.*] To continue on short route go L for a few metres to cross road and enter a permitted path on R. Cross field with river and hedge on R then cross FB on R and continue across field to follow marked path

by river bank, then along canal bank and into woods taking L fork at division in path to reach a large bridge over the canal.

Go to paragraph 4

Padworth Mill

③ Continue ahead along Fisherman's Lane to reach road at Aldermaston opposite The Hind's Head. Continue ahead along Wasing Lane, past school and turn L over stile onto FP at end of village speed restriction. After crossing 2 more stiles enter large field and head diagonally R. Go

over stile and FB and ahead over next field to FP sign post. Do not take signed FP but turn R along permitted path. Head across parkland to buildings on far side and to L of small, thatched pavilion to reach road. Turn R then, where road swings R, go ahead on FP at entrance to Wasing Lower Farm, bending R at entrance to small airfield, through hedge lined track then L to cross a bridge. Cross next field to corner of hedge opposite and, avoiding obvious track ahead, turn R through gap then L along field margin with hedge on L. At end of hedge follow FP across field then along track to road. Turn R along road to reach The Row Barge and bridge over the Kennet & Avon Canal. Turn R along towpath to reach a large bridge.

Go to paragraph 4

④ Cross bridge going ahead onto towpath on opposite bank. At road bridge, (where short cut joins), turn R across bridge then L onto towpath and follow back to start.

Walk 19

Hose Hill Lake

Start - Sheffield Bottom Lock Picnic Area Car Park.
Free, open 9.00am to dusk.
(Theale Station 1/2 mile)

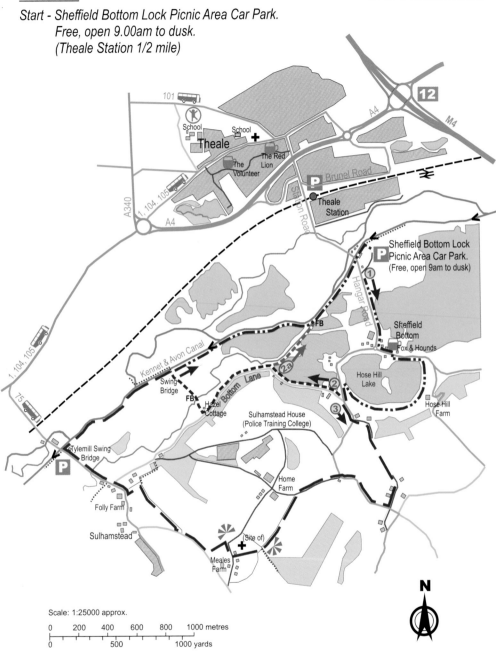

Scale: 1:25000 approx.

```
0     200    400    600    800    1000 metres
0              500              1000 yards
```

① From the car park return to the road and turn L along Hangar Road to a roundabout. Turn L and after houses on R, and opposite the Fox and Hounds pub, pass next to a barrier into Hose Hill Lake Local Nature Reserve, _(Dogs only under close control)._ Turn L and follow FP in a clockwise direction around the lake, at one point crossing the grassy area at Hose Hill Farm, then bearing R at junction to keep close to the water's edge. Shortly after passing a paddock on L turn L onto road at metal field gate, turning L again towards Bottom Lane.

Short walk - para 2   Long walk - para 3

towpath and turn R back to the start.] Otherwise continue on Bottom Lane to just past Hazel Cottage. Turn R over stile, cross a meadow, a FB and a further meadow to join the long route along the towpath back to the start.

③ Pass the end of Bottom Lane and as the road bends R take FP on L, beside high metal gates, and follow track around to R. At edge of trees go diagonally L, uphill, across field to R of pylon, heading for a house on L. Cross stile and take FP to R

Hose Hill Lake

heading up drive to road. Turn R along road and just after pylon, as road bends R, turn L along a lane. As the lane swings R to Home Farm cross stile on L onto field edge path, bearing R over stiles at top of field to cross the churchyard of a demolished church to a road. Turn R to sharp R bend then enter field ahead and turn L between fences to reach another road. Turn R downhill

② Turn R into Bottom Lane.[②ⓐ _If you have spent too much time at the nature reserve and time is pressing, follow the lane to Fisherman's Cottage, at a bend in the lane, and turn R on FP, (shown light green on map), ignoring minor paths on R, to join the_

and, at field entrance on R, take narrow field edge FP between hedges. At junction of FPs turn L across field edge and over stile by large tree on to road and turn R down road to reach the Kennet and Avon canal at Tylemill swing bridge and car park. Turn R and follow canal towpath back to the start.

Walk 20

The Dovecot

Start - Theale Station. (Car Park - Pay & Display).
Alternative Parking - Sheffield Bottom Lock Picnic Area Car Park
(free, open 9.00am to dusk).

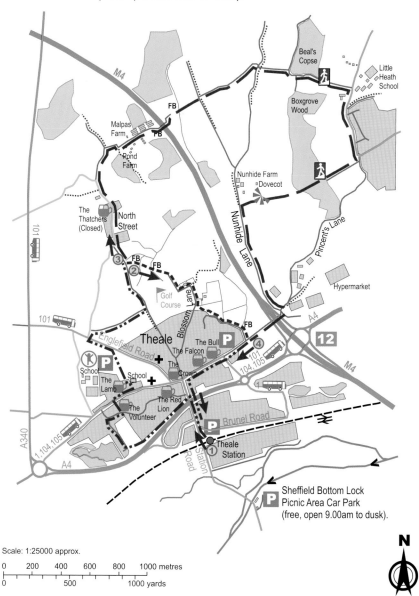

Scale: 1:25000 approx.

| 0 | 200 | 400 | 600 | 800 | 1000 metres |

| 0 | 500 | 1000 yards |

N

① Exit the car park across Brunel Road and take Station Road towards the village. Pass under Theale Bypass bridge and turn immediately L on tarmac path, passing children's play area. Where path turns towards houses continue ahead on grass track to reach wider grass area. Head for houses on far side and exit onto Volunteer Road over steps and FB. Turn R along road, at first with allotments on R and at T junction turn R into Meadow Way. Shortly after Blatch's Close take FP on L to Church Street, opposite Theale Library. Turn R and immediately after The Old Lamb Hotel take FP on L towards Theale Primary School. Turn L at school gates and follow FP around to go L across recreation ground to car park of village hall. Turn L along Englefield Road, R towards North Street then almost immediately R again on FP to golf course. At club entrance turn L on FP to reach a kissing gate on R.

Short walk - para 2   Long walk - para 3

② Turn R through kissing gate and follow clear waymark posts across golf course, (the 1st is just L of nearest large tree), being careful where FP crosses the fairways. Leave golf course at Bloom Cottage and turn R along Blossom Lane, taking FP on L across grassy area after about 100m. Where FP comes near to road take FP to L away from road, (ignore sign indicating private land and no right of way which refers to land on L of FP). Cross FB and continue ahead on narrow FP behind houses to reach road near entry barriers. Turn R.

Go to paragraph 4

③ Go straight on along FP to reach road turning R through the hamlet of North Street. Where road turns sharply L shortly after The Thatchers pub (currently closed) take "No through road" straight ahead, following it as it swings R and L to reach Malpas and Pond farms, through gate then over the FB at the M4. Go ahead over crossing path to reach Nunhide Lane near a lone house. Cross lane and head uphill. At end of field go first R then L to enter Beal's Copse, continuing on uphill FP between trees, then between fields, to reach road opposite Little Heath School. Turn R and just past Turnham's Farm Hall take FP on R at entrance to Pincent's Lane.

The Dovecot

Go downhill through wood, passing dovecot and on to Nunhide Lane. Turn L along lane and at road junction turn R and R again over FB at M4 on to track towards Theale.

Go to paragraph 4.

④ Continue on through Theale High Street and at mini roundabout near The Crown Pub turn L into Station Road and back to the start.

West Berks Ramblers is one of several groups in the Berkshire area each of which arranges its own extensive programme of activities, short local and long distance walks and walking weekends. They can be contacted at *www.wberksramblers.org.uk* or on 01635281621. All the groups belong to the national organisation, **The Ramblers**.

The Ramblers is a registered charity which promotes walking, protects rights of way, campaigns for access to the countryside and plays a major role in securing legislation to protect our environment.

ramblers
at the heart of walking

By becoming a member of **The Ramblers** you would be supporting this valuable work. You could choose which local group to join but would be free to walk with any group anywhere in Great Britain. If you would like to join us contact: *www.ramblers.org.uk*, telephone 020 7339 8501 or write to, The Ramblers, 2nd Floor, Camelford House, 87-90 Albert Embankment, London SE1 7TW.

Walk Log

Walk Number	Date Walked		Walk Number	Date Walked	
	Short	Long		Short	Long
1			11		
2			12		
3			13		
4			14		
5			15		
6			16		
7			17		
8			18		
9			19		
10			20		